First published 1992 by Bright Books Ltd/TBSL Ltd
Text and concept © Bright Books Limited, UK
Illustrations: © Colin Hollidge, UK
All rights reserved.

ISBN 1-873967-02-0

Typeset by Set Two, Ely, Cambridgeshire
Printed in Hong Kong by Wing King Tong

It doesn't matter how crowded our world becomes, nature reclaims every small space we leave empty between our business parks, roadways and housing developments.

Rabbits

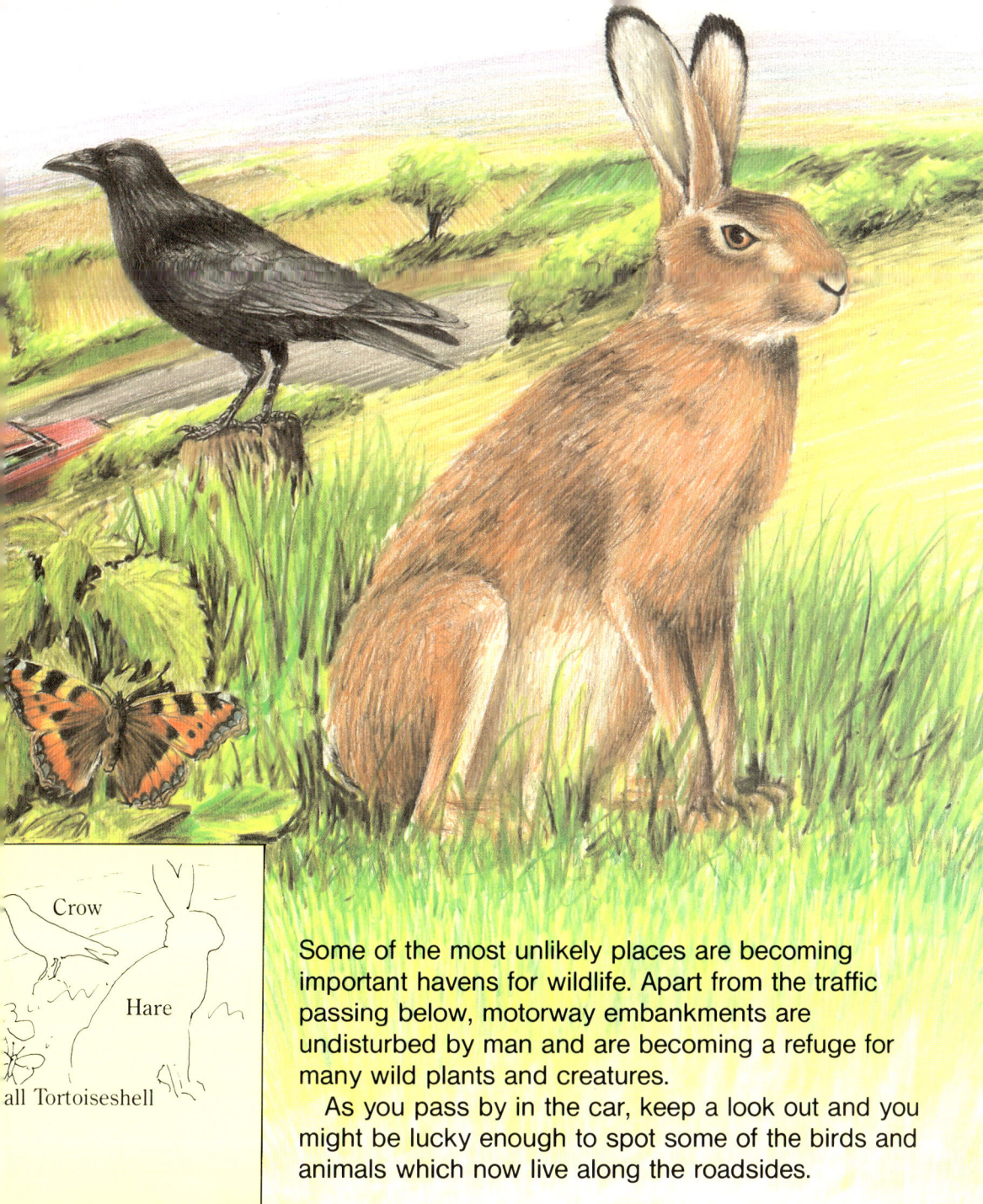

Crow
Hare
Small Tortoiseshell

Some of the most unlikely places are becoming important havens for wildlife. Apart from the traffic passing below, motorway embankments are undisturbed by man and are becoming a refuge for many wild plants and creatures.

As you pass by in the car, keep a look out and you might be lucky enough to spot some of the birds and animals which now live along the roadsides.

One of the most common birds to be seen hovering above motorway embankments is the kestrel. This member of the falcon family is highly adapted to hunting in these new habitats. In the grass below, the kestrel's sharp eyes can pick out its next meal from among the voles and mice which live on the verges.

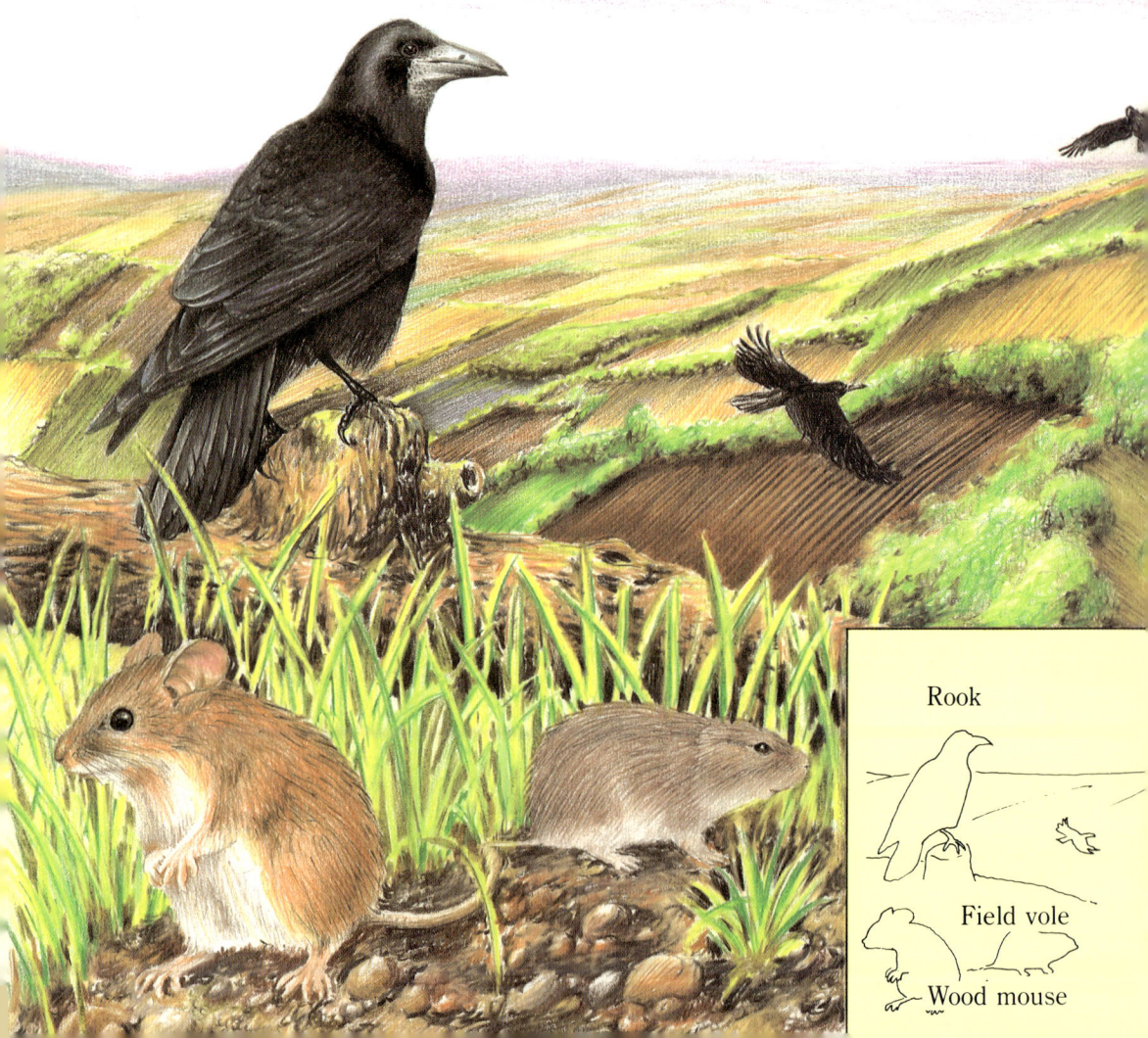

Rook

Field vole

Wood mouse

Rooks are also making the most of the 'fast food' available by the roadsides. Earthworms are brought to the surface by the rumbling of heavy traffic at certain times of day making them easy pickings for the coal-black rooks. Other scavengers, especially the rooks' cousin, the crow, take advantage of the misfortune of other animals killed while attempting to cross the carriageway.

As the development of the countryside continues for housing and for industrial use, so there are fewer 'wild' places remaining. Many butterflies depend on plants such as stinging nettles, docks and dandelions for their survival. These plants grow well in the undisturbed areas at the sides of main roads and country lanes.

Peacock

Small Copper

Nettles provide food and egg-laying sites for the Small Tortoiseshell and the Peacock butterflies. The Small Copper lays its eggs on sorrel or dock plants; the grasses themselves provide home and food for many other species from the Meadow Brown to the Small Heath butterflies.

Many trees have been planted along roadside embankments, on roundabouts and by-passes to add interest to the sometimes stark scenery. The wildlife you might spot depends on the type of trees which have been planted and how well they have grown. Where broad-leaved trees have grown into a mini-woodland, you may be able to spot the distinctive black-and-white colouring and blue-green tail of a magpie flying from treetop to treetop.

Magpies will forage among the leaf litter at the woodland fringe where hedgehogs sleep during the day. Shrews and wood mice can also be found along the tree line; these in turn attract predators such as the weasel whose long body you might see darting from one side of the road to the other.

Weasel

Wood pigeons in search of acorns and ivy berries are easy to spot, especially as they land fairly heavily in the trees, giving the branches a good bounce as they come in to land! Their pinkish chests and white wing-patches against grey feathers will help to identify them in flight.

Wood pigeons

Lapwings are starting to return to the ploughed fields of the countryside in autumn and winter. The long crest on their heads and their greenish backks with white and black markings make them easy to spot. The birds are welcomed by farmers as they eat many pests including leatherjackets and wireworms.

Lapwing

Coniferous trees in groups or plantations by the roadside or on the embankments offer a home to a different range of wildlife. Coal tits, the smallest of their family, thrive on insects found both on and beneath tree bark, and on the readily-available conifer seeds.

Grey squirrels, common in parks and gardens, have also spread through the countryside. They compete for food with the few red squirrels which survive among the conifers. Red squirrels strip the cones to get at the seeds. Grey squirrels have also found that there is a good supply of food and are moving in to take advantage of this.

In many places, especially in the centre of Britain, roads run close to rivers, canals and freshwater lakes. As well as the common mallards, moorhens and coots can be seen popping up like corks from underwater food-searching trips. In tall tree-tops beside lesser-used waterways, the population of herons is growing. Herons are very large birds, easily spotted in flight with their arched wings and legs pointing backwards well beyond their tails.

Holes seen in the bankside along the waterways are the homes of water voles, sometimes called water 'rats'. Water voles and their distant relatives the water shrews, dig out burrows in the banksides with exits on both water and land in case of emergencies. Kingfishers too nest in holes in the river banks, though as they are rare today, you would be lucky to catch a glimpse of their blue feathers flashing along the waterside.

Heron

Water shrew

Water vole

Following rivers downstream towards the sea you may find the road runs across a tidal river estuary. Here, wading birds like the oystercatcher find food among the many types of shellfish such as cockles, mussels and limpets, small crabs and worms.

Gulls make the most of the good supply of food, from fishing boats and household scraps alike, on the fringes of seaside towns and fishing ports. The herring gull and the black-headed gull are the two you are most likely to see. The herring gull is a large bird with a yellow bill sporting a red spot near the tip. The black-headed gull has many different colourings: in winter, it looks almost completely white, with dark under-wing patches and a black marking behind its eyes. In summer it shows the blackish-brown hood which gives it its name.

Oystercatcher

Only the hardiest plants, animals and birds can survive the sometimes harsh weather on moorlands and mountains. Sheep find no problem grazing steep hillsides. Further up where there are few trees, only ponies and occasional deer are to be seen roaming.

Yet amongst the bracken and colourful heathers rabbits live an under-cover life, dodging the circling birds of prey such as kestrels. In Northern Britain, twites too hide their homes among the heather, building their nests on the ground on moorland edges.

Wherever we travel, nature has something attractive and interesting to show us. But how can we help to care for the countryside, the wildlife and plants we see around us?

To help cut down the number of wild animals killed on our roads each year, conservation groups have built a variety of wildlife 'crossings': tunnels under major roads through which toads, frogs, hedgehogs and badgers can safely pass. Ramps are being put into cattle grids to help small animals climb out.

We can help by taking with us any litter left over from picnics by the roadside. Many small animals are injured while trying to get to the leftovers in plastic bags, bottles, drinks cans and yogurt pots. Using unleaded petrol and having catalytic convertors on our cars lessens the fumes which escape. Planting more trees can help us to clean up the air that we and the wildlife breathe.

the nature watch country code

Help to care for the environment in the countryside by making sure you follow the country code when you are out and about.

1. Keep the environment tidy: put your litter safely in a bin. If the litter bin on a picnic site is full, take your rubbish home.
2. Be aware and respect what's around you: don't pull bits off trees and hedgerows or test fungus on a tree stump with your feet. These things are alive and growing, just like you.
3. Leave plants in their natural habitat. Some wild flowers are very rare and must not be picked. Take a note pad and some pencils to record what you find.
4. If you want to collect 'samples' of more plentiful things such as acorns and beech nuts, take only one of any item you find: they could be important food to a small animal. Take only what has already fallen to the ground.
5. If a special nature-trail path has been made around a picnic site, camping site or wildlife reserve, stick to that path. Wandering from it could disturb wildlife and plants – and could get you into problems too.
6. Shut any gates behind you when you are out walking. There may be a reason for keeping larger animals such as sheep and cattle out of certain fields.
7. Save water where you can. Water is a necessity not just to us but to the wildlife and plants around us. Don't waste it!
8. When camping – and also at home! – use products which do not harm the earth and which break down quickly and harmlessly in the environment.
9. Never take home a 'pet' such as a frog, toad, grasshopper or cricket. These creatures belong where you find them in their homes: not yours.
10. Let everyone know you care for the environment by helping them to follow the country code too.

for young people

✪WATCH is the junior wing of the largest voluntary organisation in the UK concerned with all aspects of wildlife protection – the RSNC Wildlife Trusts Partnership. Through its **WATCH Trust for Environmental Education, sponsored by The Sunday Times, the Partnership adopts an innovative and participative approach to education and the environment. WATCH** is administered from the headquarters of the Royal Society for Nature Conservation, The Green, Witham Park, Lincoln LN5 7JR, UK.

for parents

✪WATCH is a national club for young people who care about wildlife and the environment as a whole. You don't have to be a certain age to join and it's fun to be a member. You can take part in national projects such as monitoring ozone in the air, finding out about acid rain, surveying bats, frogs and toads and many other species. You can become an active local conservationist: there are **WATCH** groups throughout the UK helping to increase our knowledge of the world around us.

WATCH members receive a membership card, badge, and copies of **WATCH-WORD**, the colourful, information-packed magazine published each school holiday. You will receive information about national activities and a newsletter giving details of your local **WATCH** group's events.

how to join

Fill in and detach the form, cutting along the line provided. Send it with your subscription to the address on the form. Subscription rates are accurate at the time of printing this edition: January 1992. For up-to-date subscription rates please telephone: UK 0522 544400.

join ✲WATCH now!

To: **WATCH**: The Green, Witham Park, Lincoln LN5 7JR.
Please enrol as new members of **WATCH**:

Name(s) _____ Date(s) of birth _____

Address _____

_____

The subscription is £5 per member, (£12 for 3 years) or £8 (£18 for 3 years) for up to four children of the same family living at one address. Adults may enrol as Associates of WATCH for an annual subscription of £10.

I enclose cheque/postal order for £ .... in payment of the subscription due

Signed _____ Date _____

Address (if different from above) _____

_____

This page may be freely photocopied, but for all other pages all rights are strictly reserved by the publisher.